BEN'S FANTASTIC PLANT

Pamela Oldfield

Illustrated by Sholto Walker

One day a parcel came for Ben.

"It's the smallest parcel I've ever seen," said the postman. It fitted easily into the palm of Ben's hand. He stared at it.

"Whatever can it be?" Dad wondered. Slowly Ben unwrapped the parcel. Inside was a big blue seed.

There was a letter, too, from his uncle in Borneo.

Dear Ben,
This is the seed from a fantastic plant. I found it growing in the jungle with lots of other plants. I was walking underneath it and this seed fell right into my hands. I thought you might like to grow it in a pot.

"How exciting," cried Mum. She helped Ben to find a pot and he planted the blue seed carefully.

"All the way from Borneo!" he said. "I hope the plant will be happy here."

That evening Ben put the pot beside his bed and went to sleep.

The next morning, he woke up to feel something tickling his face. The seed had grown very fast during the night. It was now a huge plant with bright green leaves!

"Amazing!" cried Mum.

"Astonishing!" cried Dad.

"Fantastic!" cried Ben.

Mum said, "Take it to school and show your teacher."

The teacher and the children watched in amazement as the plant went on growing.

Miss Bray said, "I can hardly believe it. It's incredible!"

The other children were excited, but Ben was a little worried. The bright green leaves drooped sadly. The branches seemed to be reaching out for something.

"It looks unhappy," Ben thought. "Perhaps it wants to be in the jungle with all the other plants. Perhaps it misses them."

By the next day, the plant was growing all over the classroom. News of the fantastic plant spread and soon a young man arrived at the school. He was a reporter and he worked for a local newspaper. They showed him the plant and Ben explained.

"My uncle sent a big blue seed from Borneo. He was walking in the jungle and it fell right into his hands." The reporter scribbled excitedly in his notebook, but Ben was still worried.

"I think the plant wants to go home. It looks unhappy," he told him. "It doesn't like living in a classroom."

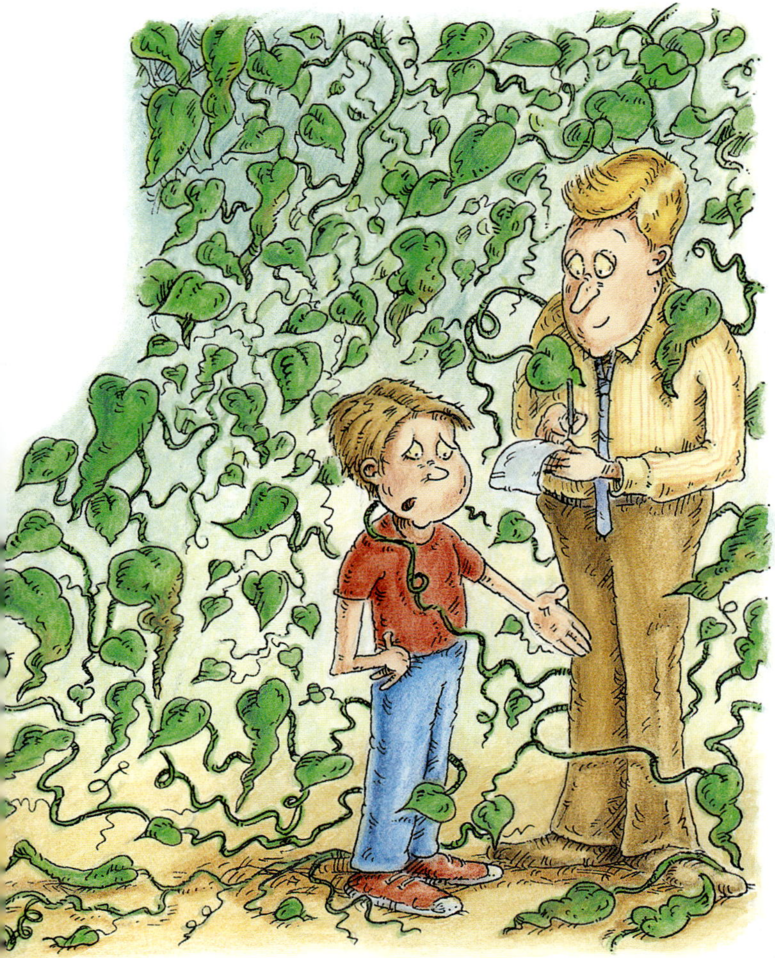

The next day, Dad showed the newspaper to Ben.

"It's all about your fantastic plant!" he told Ben. "The plant is quite famous now."

But Ben sighed. "It's growing too big," he said. "I think it's trying to get home."

An expert on rare plants also read about Ben's plant in the newspaper. His name was Septimus Clark and he came rushing down to the school with his camera.

He took hundreds of photographs from every angle. Now yellow buds were beginning to appear among the leaves. Septimus Clark was very excited.

"This plant only produces one seed," he told Ben. "It grows in the jungle with hundreds of other plants. It is very rare. It only likes to live in the jungle with lots of other plants."

Ben said, "That's why it's unhappy. It misses them. It wants to go home." But no one would listen.

The fantastic plant grew and grew until it was too big for the school. Ben wanted to send the plant back to Borneo, but no one would listen to him.

Septimus Clark took it away and put it under a huge glass dome. It was all alone.

"We'll look after it for you," he told Ben, but Ben was still worried.

The plant was so famous it couldn't even grow in peace. The television people made a programme about it.

There were chat shows and phone-ins about it. Radio commentators talked about it. The newspapers were full of articles about it.

One day Ben decided to visit his fantastic plant in its new home under the glass.

"The buds have opened!" cried Ben. The plant was covered with beautiful yellow flowers, but it still looked unhappy. Ben put his arms around the stem and felt it tremble. Suddenly drops of water fell from the plant. They were just like tears. Ben hugged the plant.

"Don't worry," he told it. "I'll think of something."

He rushed home and wrote a letter.

> Dear Uncle,
> The plant is unhappy here. Its leaves are drooping. It misses the jungle. It wants to go home. Please come and take it back to Borneo.
>
> Love from Ben.

After he had written the letter, he felt happier. Soon the plant would be going home. He stuck on a stamp and hurried off to post the letter.

On Saturday, he went to see the plant again. He wanted to tell it the good news. But – oh dear! Before he could say a word, a yellow petal fluttered to the ground. Then another. Soon the petals were falling all around him.

"Oh no!" cried Ben. Septimus Clark came along and they stood together among the falling petals. At last Ben asked the dreadful question.

"Is the plant dying?"

The expert looked thoughtful.

"Maybe," he said, "but don't worry, Ben. It will give us another seed and we can grow another plant."

"Another unhappy plant!" thought Ben. He couldn't bear to think about it.

The next day, a letter came from Ben's uncle.

> Dear Ben,
> I am so sorry about the plant. I will come and fetch it as soon as I can, but I am very busy just now.

Ben went back to the plant.

"It won't be long now," he told it. "My uncle will take you back to the jungle as soon as he can."

By now the plant was growing out of the top of its glass dome. Leaves and petals were falling like snow.

Two days later, a sudden storm blew up out of nowhere. Black clouds filled the sky and thunder rumbled.

Suddenly – disaster! The top of the plant was struck by a very bright flash of lightning! At once the stem twisted. The remaining leaves and flowers withered.

Someone fetched Septimus Clark, but it was already too late. Septimus Clark sent for Ben.

"Oh no!" cried Ben and he hugged the plant again. If his uncle came now he would be too late. The leaves and petals fell, leaving the stem bare and twisted.

21

Ben looked up at it with tears in his eyes. It was all over. But at that very moment something fell from the plant, right into his hands! It was a big blue seed!

Quick as a flash, Ben slipped it

into his pocket. Then he looked round cautiously. Had Septimus Clark seen what had happened? No. Ben breathed a sigh of relief. The seed was safe. Ben winked at the plant.

"It's our secret," he whispered.

Poor Septimus Clark was searching frantically.

"We must find the seed," he told Ben. "Then we can grow another plant."

"Of course!" said Ben, looking very innocent. "I'll help you to look for it."

He pretended to search, scrabbling among the fallen petals, peering under each dead leaf. Septimus Clark had no idea that the big blue seed was safely hidden in Ben's pocket.

Ben was feeling cheerful again. He knew exactly what he would do.

That evening, he found some wrapping paper. He smiled at the big blue seed.

"I'm sending you home," he told it. "You can grow in the jungle with all the other plants. You'll have all the space you want and you'll be happy there."

Then Ben wrote to his uncle to tell him what had happened. He folded the letter very small and wrapped it up with the seed. He didn't tell anyone. Not Mum. Not Dad.

The next day, on his way home from school, Ben took the parcel to the post office.

"Good gracious!" said the man behind the counter. "It's the smallest parcel I've ever seen. Whatever is it? What are you sending to Borneo?"

Ben smiled, but shook his head.

"It's a secret," he said.

The next day, Miss Bray said, "You're looking cheerful today, Ben."

Ben smiled. He did not dare to tell anyone why he was feeling so happy. He kept thinking about the seed on its way to Borneo.

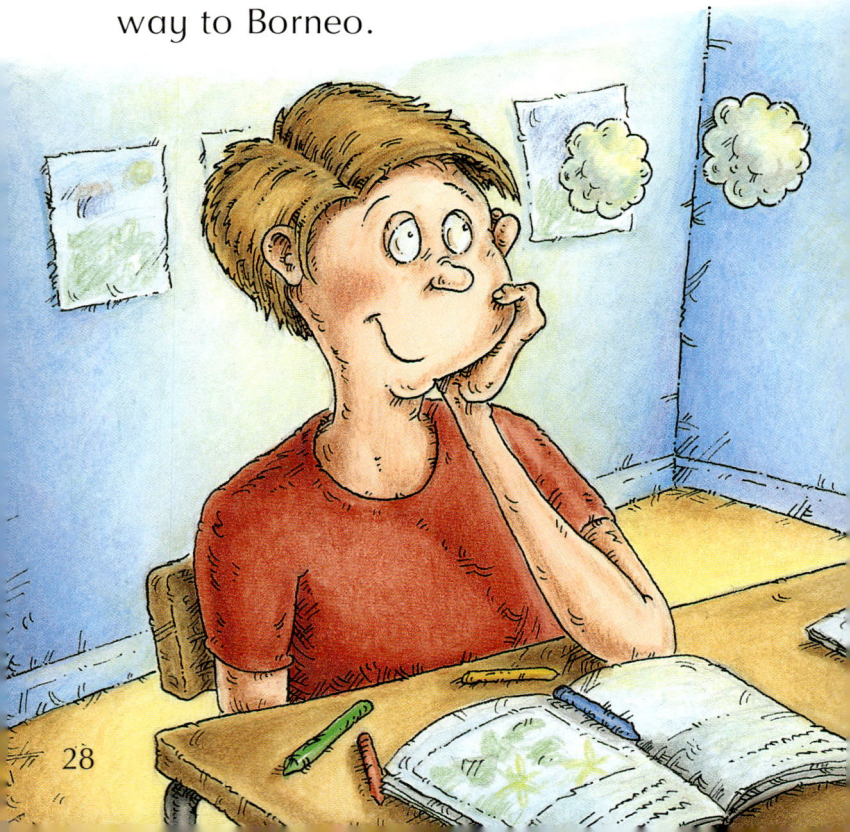

A long, long way away, in Borneo, Ben's uncle opened the tiny parcel.

"Blow me down!" he said. Then he read Ben's letter. "Oh dear! How very sad. The fantastic plant died." He looked at the big blue seed which lay in the palm of his hand. "I'm sorry," he told it. "I made a big mistake, sending that seed so far from home."

He put on some big boots and collected a spade. Then he set off for the nearest jungle and planted the seed.

"You'll be happy there, with all the other plants," he said. As he walked away two green leaves pushed their way out of the ground. The new fantastic plant was already growing.

A week later, Septimus Clark was being interviewed on the television.

"It's a complete mystery," he grumbled. "We've searched for the big blue seed, but it seems to have vanished. So now, of course, we can't grow another plant."

"Good!" said Ben. He smiled a happy, secret smile. In his mind's eye he could see the new fantastic plant with its bright green leaves and bright yellow flowers. It was growing in the jungle with all the other plants, where it belonged.